IT CAN GET BETTER...

Dealing with common behaviour problems in
young children with autism

A GUIDE FOR PARENTS AND CARERS

Paul Dickinson and Liz Hannah

With illustrations by
Steve Lockett

The National Autistic Society

First published 1998 (reprinted 2000, 2005 and 2007) by
The National Autistic Society
393 City Road
London
EC1V 1NG

ISBN 978 1 899280 0 32
Copyright © The National Autistic Society
Designed by Cottier & Sidaway Design Partnership
Printed in Great Britain by Crowes Complete Print

Contents

Acknowledgements

Acknowledgements

Thanks to eveyone who has helped us prepare this booklet. Thanks especially to Steve for his wonderful drawings and his patience while we've both struggled to get this done in between all the other things we try and do. Thanks to Jacquie Turner who read through a draft script from a parent's perspective and also to Mrs D Turnbull-Justice. We also thank The National Autistic Society for agreeing to print and publish our work and for supporting our aim of trying to produce something useful for parents. Above all, thanks to the children we have worked with, and their parents who first put to us that writing this was something we should do.

Introduction

Over the years that we have both been working with children with the complex, disabling and bewildering condition called autism, we have found their dedicated but worried families frequently coming to us for advice about particular behavioural problems. The themes have been ongoing: trials over toilet training, long lasting temper tantrums, obsessive rituals that can seem to enslave families, and sometimes frustrations that are expressed by frightening acts of self-injury.

Often we have both wished we could give parents a book that was written for them, containing not complicated programmes more appropriate for professionals, but rather practical hints that might help them through a difficult period and which they could turn to when they needed to tackle some of the day to day challenges of caring for a child with this special type of 'special need'.

We had also thought it would be good for parents and carers to be given some tips early on. All too often children come to our attention after they have already started school. Professionals from education, health and perhaps social services have been busy with assessments, and contributing to Statements of Special Educational Needs. Sometimes people cope too well. They struggle on until their child's difficult behaviour patterns become very well established and hard to change. If someone had been able to sit down with the child's parents earlier to go through some basic ideas of how to cope with certain situations, or if there had been something written down they could have to take away......

We do not claim to possess expertise that will enable you to respond to every difficult situation that you may find yourself in. What we have tried to do in this booklet is to pull together the tips and ideas that appear to have helped people in our respective work over the years. We have also sought to share the practical ways of coping that parents we have known have come up with themselves, and then shared generously with us, and also with others who are going through similar experiences. These are things that cannot be read in any professional textbook, but come from the unique experience of being the parent or carer of an autistic child.

We hope this booklet helps you to feel more positive about your ability to respond to the challenges that go with being the parent of an autistic child.

Paul Dickinson   **Liz Hannah**

Some general pointers

- Whatever strategy you decide to use, break it down into manageable steps. Take it stage by stage and concentrate on one step at a time.

- You have to be patient. When you start a behaviour programme with your child it may take up to six weeks before there is any great improvement.

- You have to be consistent. Decide what you are going to do and stick to it for six to eight weeks. Make sure that other people who are with your child, including school staff, grandparents and friends all do the same thing.

'Oh by the way mum, we're rewarding good behaviour and ignoring bad'

- Don't worry if things get worse to begin with. That is a normal reaction when children want things to stay the same and try harder to see that they do.

- It may help to keep a diary and write in it from time to time. It is reassuring to look back and see that progress has been made. Because it happens slowly, it is sometimes easy to forget what things were like at the beginning.

- Get as much support as possible! Don't be afraid to talk to your health visitor or your child's teacher who should be working with you on these issues and may be able to get help for you from other sources if things are particularly difficult.

- Whatever strategies you decide to use will depend on your child and your family. You have to choose a plan that is realistic and is not going to cause you more upset and frustration than the behaviour you are trying to change.

- Think carefully about activities, items of food and other things your child really enjoys and use these as rewards and distractions. Changing your child's behaviour can be difficult at times but it is enormously rewarding when progress is made.

1 Dealing with temper tantrums

Introduction

Many children have temper tantrums when they are young. It is not uncommon to see a red-faced, harassed parent loaded up with shopping, struggling with a screaming, kicking, furious child. However when the child is bigger and stronger the situation becomes more difficult and it is often easier to give the child what they want in order to stop the disruption, especially when it feels as though the whole street is watching. The result is that the child gains a lot of attention and learns that by having a tantrum they will finally get what they want.

Situations like this can be very intimidating so it is important to feel confident that you are in control. Children have temper tantrums for a number of reasons and it is important when looking for the best solution to try and understand why your child is behaving in this way. It may be something obvious, for example they once had chocolate while shopping so now they want it every time. If it is not so obvious, or your child has a lot of tantrums for a number of reasons, try writing down all the situations in which they occur for a couple of weeks. Note down the time of day, what triggered the behaviour and what happened as a result. Then look at all the information you have gathered and see if there is any pattern. What you want to find out is what your child gains by having a tantrum. When you know this, you can look for a way of dealing with it successfully.

The tantrum may be attention seeking

If you respond to your child's tantrums by cajoling, shouting, trying to comfort, or punishing, you are giving your child a lot of attention when they present this behaviour. It doesn't matter to the child that you are angry because they soon learn that if they want all your attention then all they have to do is have a temper tantrum.

- Instead of giving attention to bad behaviour, give lots of praise when your child is behaving well or playing quietly.

- Don't give attention when your child is having a tantrum. If necessary turn your back, carry on doing something else, go to the toilet, wash the dishes or just look the other way. Some children may try to gain your attention by pulling at your clothes, kicking or hitting you or being destructive. If this is impossible to ignore, tell the child calmly they are going to their room (or any safe place) until they have calmed down. Then leave them. If you are worried, you can always listen at the door to make sure they are OK.

Go to your room

- Give lots of praise and comfort when the tantrum is over.

- When children learn that they get attention by having a tantrum, they will try even harder to get that attention when the tantrum is ignored. It is important to remember this and work through it. The behaviour will often get worse before it gets better.

If the tantrums began after the birth of a new baby make sure that you involve your child as much as possible in helping you care for the baby and give lots of praise for helpful and good behaviour. Try to find some time each day to

It's alright, he just wants our attention

spend with your older child doing something special you can enjoy together. It is also important to encourage visitors to give attention to older children and not only to the baby.

The tantrum occurs when the child is told 'No'

- It is difficult for young children to understand why they can't have everything they want. It is even more difficult for children with autism to understand, particularly when things are unpredictable. For example, sometimes they have something for a treat and at other times the treat is not available or not allowed. In these occasions it is very important to be consistent. It is tempting (and will sometimes be necessary) to give in because you are tired, everybody is staring, and you just want to get away as quickly as possible. However, try to work out a strategy in advance and stick to it.

- If your child thinks that passing a MacDonalds without buying anything is totally unacceptable it may be necessary to practice walking past MacDonalds on quiet days when you have someone with you to help. Just walk boldly past saying firmly 'no MacDonalds today'. It will also be important to avoid passing MacDonalds with your child if you don't feel you can cope with a struggle, and for a few weeks or even months it may be a good idea to avoid going in to MacDonalds and similar places altogether.

- Make it clear to your child that you understand why they are angry but be very consistent in how you respond.

- Ignore the tantrum if you can. Don't feel guilty or feel that you are a terrible parent because your child is screaming and sobbing for something you have said 'no' to. It is even more important not to show them that you are feeling uncomfortable and might change your mind. They'll get over it and sometimes they learn amazingly quickly that you mean what you say.

- Don't be angry or punish your child for their behaviour; it will make the situation more difficult and won't solve the problem in the long run. Try to keep calm and give lots of praise when your child is calmer.

- If possible, you could try to distract your child. However children with autism can be extremely difficult to distract when they particularly want something.

- Shopping may be just too much for some children to cope with. The range of food on the shelves, the colours and the sounds can overstimulate children with autism and they may find the whole experience very difficult. If this is the case, go supermarket shopping when your child is at school or playgroup. Then when you are feeling more relaxed take them to a smaller shop for just one or two items and try to make it a pleasurable occasion. Give lots of praise and a small reward if they manage the outing well. Be careful when choosing a reward, take it in your bag rather than buy it in the shop. Otherwise, you could make the situation worse unless you are willing to buy the same reward each time you go shopping.

- At home it is often easier to simply keep things out of reach and out of sight if the child is constantly wanting things that are not allowed.

The tantrum occurs when the child wants to avoid something unpleasant

- Your child may have a tantrum in order to avoid doing something that is necessary, eg having a bath. In this case it is best to work out a routine that suits you and follow it every day. Keep the bath short at first and reward your child at the end by giving them an activity or food reward they enjoy. If you think your child is really frightened of the bath, you will need to break the process down into small steps. For example:

Week 1: A quick strip wash by the basin. (If it is summer, you could also gently encourage water play in the garden at suitable opportunities.)
Week 2: Stand in the empty bath for a few minutes with a favourite toy or treat, then get out and have a quick strip wash.
Week 3: Have a quick strip wash while standing in the empty bath.
Week 4: Put a small amount of water in the bath and have a quick wash.
Week 5,6,7: Increase the amount of water in the bath and the amount of time in the bath.

Bathtime

The tantrum is a method of communication

Some children have tantrums because they are unable to communicate what they want or cannot express their feelings. They may also have difficulty understanding what they are being told. It is therefore necessary to work with your child's teacher or with a speech and language therapist to develop a communication system for your child using signs, symbols or photographs that will support spoken language and gestures. It is also important, when giving instructions, to keep your language clear and brief and to emphasise the most important words.

② Toileting problems

Introduction

Dr Christopher Green who wrote the popular book for parents, *Toddler Taming**, said that toileting was one of the areas where children have the ultimate veto. If a child goes rigid and refuses to sit on the potty, then all attempts to convince, or coerce them to bend in the middle and sit will be in vain.

What applies to ordinary children applies just as much to autistic children and more so. In addition to all the normal challenges of toilet training, autistic children:

- often have learning difficulties, so it may take them much longer to learn the basic skills needed for them to go to the toilet independently. It can take up to a year and sometimes more for autistic children to become dry, and two years or more for them to become clean

* Green, C (1992) *Toddler Taming*. Vermilion, London.

- often have problems learning to speak and to use language. They may not be able to tell you they need the toilet in words so you have to look out for other signs that they need to go

Do you want a
wee wee?

- may find it hard to adapt from one situation to another. Because of this they may go to the toilet quite happily at home but need nappies at nursery or school. If someone tries to take them to the toilet at school they may become very upset and have temper tantrums
- may become clean, or dry but not both. Sometimes autistic children will quite happily urinate in the toilet, but refuse to sit on the toilet to defecate. They may worry about getting splashed with water
- may develop difficult patterns of behaviour around going to the toilet such as smearing faeces on the walls of the toilet, elsewhere or on themselves. Sometimes this is a particular problem at nightime
- may do a wee or a poo in other places as well as the toilet. They do not seem to realise this is often completely inappropriate.

- may refuse to clean themselves after having a poo because they become very upset at the thought of becoming messy or dirty in any way. For some autistic children this fear means that they refuse to move their bowels at all and they become badly constipated, and suffer from bad tummy pains and other symptoms.
- sometimes can hurt themselves by pulling at their genitals or digging at themselves either at night or when they go to the toilet

Your little boy or girl may have one of these problems, a combination of them, or maybe none. But if toileting is a difficulty, read on.

Learning difficulties, autism and toileting

As with any skill, how easily toileting is learned depends on how mild or severe your child's autism is and how mild or severe their learning difficulties are. Toileting difficulties are, however, very common for children with autism. A survey conducted by one of our colleagues found that 82% of the children in her study had difficulties, or had previously experienced difficulties with toileting.*

* Szyndler, J (1996) 'Toileting problems in a group of children with autism' *Child Psychology and Psychiatry Review 1(1).*

Your child's autism means they often have great difficulty in understanding the social rules governing our lives – why shouldn't they strip off and have a wee in the middle of the park if they need to?

If your child also has learning difficulties it may take them much longer to learn any skill. They may also take a long time to learn their bodies' signals. They may not realise they really need to go.

How do I begin to tackle this problem?

Two things that any parent needs in abundance:

- patience
- a sense of humour

Both of these are hard to come by at times. If you can hang on to these qualities however it may do a lot for your sanity in the longer term.

- First of all don't try and make a battle of toileting with your child; you probably won't win and things may get worse.

Don't make it a battle

- To tackle any toileting problem you will probably need to go one step at a time.

- Expect things to take longer than they would with children who do not suffer from autism or have learning difficulties.

- You are not alone. Most parents of autistic children will have gone through some aspect of what you will be going through.

- There are people who can help. If you find yourself at a loss about how to tackle this area, you may be able to turn to a number of different people for support and advice:
    - Your GP or paediatrician
    - A clinical child psychologist (your doctor or health visitor can refer you)
    - The local branch of The National Autistic Society. You can meet other parents there who may well have ideas that have worked for them and which might help you. They also really do know 'what it's like' and that can be a comfort.
    - Your child's school or nursery. If your child goes to a special school or nursery for children with learning difficulties, or a school for autistic children, staff may well have a lot of experience in teaching toileting skills. You may be able to talk to them about things they are trying at school that you can try at home too. That can be effective because it means the problem is being tackled consistently.

Going for help

If you go and seek professional advice you need to be honest about what you can do and cannot do. That way the person who is working with you can try and tailor the advice they give to your circumstances. Very often when we go and seek advice about some aspect of being a parent we go out of our way to create a good impression, because we don't want our seeking help to be viewed as a sign of being a bad parent. That often comes from the feeling that we are to blame for the problem. Parents sometimes do make mistakes, but no-one teaches us how to be a parent, especially not how to be the parent of a child with special needs.

If you are feeling tired or down, or your confidence is at a low ebb, try and be honest about this with the professional you're seeing.

PARENT GUIDANCE

It may be that initially what's needed is some support for you as a parent to get you through a tough patch. Once you're feeling better in yourself you may be able to tackle the problem with more confidence, and confidence in your abilities as a parent is often part of the solution. The person who is working with you may be able to help you directly or explore various avenues where you can get support. There are a number of helplines around that you can phone when there isn't anyone else to talk to (see 'Useful organisations' for helpline numbers).

Strategies to try

There is no magic wand, and these strategies are not formulas guaranteed to produce results every time. You may find your own solution in time, but we've put down some ideas that we've used in our work and that have helped parents in the past. Above all, you have to be realistic. There is no point trying to implement some strategy that in the end you can't follow through because it takes more energy and commitment than you have to spare – you'll just end up frustrated and maybe angry and depressed.

1 Establishing a routine

Like any child, an autistic child can be helped to get into 'good habits'. Take them to sit on the toilet or the potty after every meal. After meals is a good time because the gut naturally seems to try and 'make room' for the new food to be digested by pushing waste out. Try taking your child about 20 minutes after a meal. Getting the timing right will be a matter of trial and error!

2 Look out for signals

Your child may give out particular non-verbal signals that they want a wee or a poo. These can be very varied; children can fidget in a particular way or go to a certain place (one little boy I knew would go and hide under a table when he was about to do a poo!). Try and respond to these signals by taking the child to the toilet and encouraging them to sit on the toilet or potty. Try and get them to sit for a short period of time, say five minutes, before you let them off. If they don't do anything let them off but take them back a short time later, especially if they give signals that they are about to do something in a nappy or their pants.

3 Prompting

Many children without learning difficulties who have 'lazy bowels' or suffer from incontinence need prompting to go to the toilet to avoid accidents. This is just as important if not more so for children with autism as they may not recognise their body's signals telling them they need the toilet.

4 Rewards

Showing your child that you are pleased when they use the toilet or potty properly can be quite powerful. Just because a child is autistic doesn't mean they are not interested in praise or small treats. For some children praise will be most effective; for others being allowed to do some favourite activity, or being given something nice to eat. You will discover what works best as a reward for your child.

Well done sweetie!

5 Don't encourage rituals

Some children will try and insist that specific rituals are undertaken when going to the toilet. Try not to go along with these for the sake of a quiet life. If you do, things can become more difficult in the long run.

Special aids for more difficult problems

Some children have particular problems learning to be clean and dry and sometimes special aids can help.

Alarms

A special pad is put under the sheets (if the problem is night wetting or soiling) or in the child's pants. If your child starts to wet, this triggers a buzzer or a bell. For children who wet the bed this usually wakes them up and they seem to automatically 'hold on' and stop wetting. These alarms are usually given out by doctors at special clinics for toileting problems, or psychologists who will explain exactly how they should be used. There are also special buzzers that can be put inside a potty to help teach your child to use it properly. Alarms are often effective when used alongside 'behavioural programmes' designed to help you teach your child.

Mattress covers

If wet beds are a big problem special covers to protect the mattress are available from either specialist clinics or sometimes through your health visitor. Clinics and your health visitor may also be able to get other 'incontinence aids' to help you keep the washing down to a more reasonable level until the problem improves. If your local child development service has a special needs health visitor they might be a good person to ask for information about this.

Night suits

Some children have particular behavioural problems around toileting. One especially distressing difficulty is when children 'smear' poo. They may do this at night in particular. If this is the case you can get special suits for children to wear at night which stop them from doing this or hurting themselves by scratching or digging at their bottoms. (Don't worry, it's not like putting them in some kind of 'straitjacket'.)

Mattress covers and sleep suits that help prevent smearing and other special aids may be available through a variety of NHS services. Your local special needs health visitor may be the first person to contact to find out more. They will often be able to organise supplies of nappies for children who are delayed in achieveing continence as a first step. Agencies like MENCAP (see under Useful organisations for phone number) may also be able to advise what might be available and how to go about getting it. Many local health services have 'Enuresis clinics' for example which may be able to provide help and advice. The way in to these services may also be through your health visitor or GP.

Medication
Sometimes medication can help if your child suffers from constipation or wets either at night or during the day. Your own GP or paediatrician can advise you about this.

What if my child seems afraid of the toilet?

This is a common problem particularly in more able and verbal children. Try taking things in stages to overcome this problem. For example, if your child normally uses a nappy:

- try and get them to wee or poo in the nappy but while they are in the toilet
- then try to get them to sit on the toilet with the lid down while they are still wearing their nappy
- then move on to sitting with the lid up and undressed
- finally with no nappy and wiping themselves.

This is just an example. A psychologist or other professional helper could work with you on a special programme for your child. It will be important though, for you to take your child regularly and for you to try and remain calm. Remember that change may be slow.

If your little boy or girl is afraid of getting messy or dirty, playing with things like play dough, finger paints, pastry and clay can help reduce their fears. This may teach them that becoming messy is not the end of the world as you can always get clean again.

Summary

If we tried to cover every possible strategy or programme for every kind of toileting problem that would take a booklet all of its own! You may find that patience, gentle encouragement, and perseverance will in the end pay dividends. Remember, many parents find it takes quite a while. Above all:

- don't be frightened to ask for help, especially with distressing problems like smearing. The fact that there is a problem doesn't mean it's your fault

- children with more severe learning difficulties may need special training programmes in place for a while to help them become clean and dry. You can get help with this

- for some children staying clean and dry is a matter of being taken regularly and reminded that they need to go

- really bad toileting problems are no joke – get support, help and advice if you need it.

③ Sleep problems

Introduction

Sleep problems are very common in autistic children. There can be a number of different reasons why they find it hard to go to bed or to sleep. Here are some possibilities:

- fear of the dark
- fear of being left alone
- hyperactivity
- difficulty in moving from one activity to another, for example watching a favourite video to getting ready for bed.

Very often it is not the child who has a sleep problem (they often appear to need less, or they simply catch up at other times) but the parents. It is the parents who regularly have dark rings around their eyes and look shellshocked!

It is good to get your child into a proper routine at bedtime, and it's very important for you to get a decent night's sleep. If you get overtired you can become impatient, irritable and quick to get cross. Problems that might be bearable at other times can quickly become too much to cope with when you haven't had enough sleep.

Common problems

Bedtime tantrums

These can work very well for a child as they occur when parents may themselves be looking forward to some peace and quiet, and may be feeling tired themselves. It can seem easier to let a child stay up longer, play for a few more minutes, or watch a favourite video.

As with all the problems, it is important to think what the child may be trying to tell you through their behaviour.

A child might be telling you that they are anxious, or afraid. Or that they are hungry, or simply not tired. If a child is afraid of the dark or of being alone, there may be some very simple things that can be changed to improve things:

- have a night light
- move your child in with a brother or sister
- leave their bedroom door slightly ajar so that they can hear your voices, or hear you moving about the house
- have a tape recorder to play quiet and soothing music.

There may be some other practical things that you can do which might be helpful:

- make sure your child's bedroom is comfortable and friendly
- have favourite toys, objects and pictures of favourite things in the room
- have warm bedclothes
- make sure your child is not hungry before they go to bed
- have a regular bedtime routine and stick to it.

Lack of routine

Children with autism need routines to help them cope with a world they find frightening and where they often cannot work out what may happen next. It is important that home and school life doesn't contain too many surprises in the course of a day. Bedtimes need to be regular. The build up to bedtime needs to happen in the same way, if at all possible, each night. For example:

7.20 pm
- Offer small drink
- Get pyjamas on
- Clean teeth
- Go to toilet

- Kiss family goodnight
- Get favourite soft toy
- Go to bed

Things may not be organised in exactly the same way in your house, but it is important to have a routine. You must be firm however hard this is – if you give in, you are rewarding challenging behaviour. The more you give in, the harder it will be to change the behaviour in the long run.

It may be important to have a nice, rewarding activity ready for your child when they get into bed like a short story.

Once you have followed your bedtime routine LEAVE THE ROOM.

Try very hard not to go back in to your child's room if they have a tantrum. You must try to ignore it. Remember you may be trying to change your child's behaviour, but they are aiming to change yours! If you go back in the room and let them out of bed, they will have successfully changed your behaviour in the direction they want.

But what happens if they get out of bed and come out of their room?

There is only one way to handle this – take them back without fuss or comment (the without fuss bit is very important).

My child has violent tantrums, throwing and breaking things if we make him stay in his bedroom

Okay, we admit this is a tough one, but there are ways to tackle this – childproof the room.

- Remove easily breakable toys, put in lots of soft toys (you can even find rubber bricks in some joke shops!) which your child can throw around if they feel really angry.

- Make sure the wall paper has no loose edges your child can use to rip chunks of it off the walls if they are feeling angry. Perhaps think about getting some of that wall paper you can paint over if necessary.

- Sometimes parents have found putting a small catch on the door helpful which prevents the child from completely leaving the room, while allowing them to see out. This may prevent you or your partner from having to do 'guard duty' outside the bedroom door to return your escaping child.

We are not suggesting you lock your child in their room, this may make them frightened. If a child continually gets out of the room you may have to stay outside the room for a while to put them back into bed quickly. If there are two of you, it may be helpful to take turns at this until things settle down a bit, and the child gets the message that they have to go to bed and stay there.

All children have to learn that being put to bed is not the end of the world, and actually going to bed can be very nice. Having a firm and consistent routine is the best way to get your child to learn this. It is important also to make bedtime a quiet and soothing time. Common sense tells us not to get a child overexcited with rough and tumble play just before bedtime.

When thinking about bedtimes it is important to be realistic; all children are different, some need a lot more sleep than others. Some children also have naps in addition to sleep at night. If your child has a two hour nap in the afternoon and then bounces around until the wee small hours, it may be worth cutting down on their daytime sleeps.

Hyperactivity

Some children with autism are hyperactive. Although there is a group of children in the general population who suffer from hyperactivity, this condition is more common in children with autism and those with learning disabilities. In its most extreme form doctors sometimes give this condition the name hyperkinetic syndrome or hyperkinetic disorder. 'Hyperkinetic' comes from old Greek meaning 'too much' or 'over' and 'movement' or 'motion'. If your child seems to survive on very little sleep (I saw one little boy who regularly got by on five hours or less a night and no daytime sleeps), it may be worth consulting your GP or paediatrician. Medication can be helpful in some (but not all) cases. Sometimes medication and a behavioural sleep programme worked out by a psychologist can help you make changes.

Sleeping in Mum and Dad's bed

Where children sleep when they are very little really varies. Not only families, but cultures have very different rules about children sleeping with parents. In Japan for example it is normal for a baby to sleep between its mother and father at first. If your young child sleeps with you and it doesn't bother you that's fine but if it does bother you that's different.

What can be troubling to parents is when a child gets into a habit of sleeping in their bed over a number of years. It's one thing if a toddler comes into your bed, but an 11 year old is a different matter. Many families have in the back of their minds a time when they believe a child should be in their own bed. If you are looking towards that time then maybe it would be an idea to think about how you are going to make the change smoothly.

First of all why might your child not want to sleep in their own bed? There could be a number of reasons: fear of the dark, feeling cold at night, not feeling very well, feeling a bit insecure. A few small changes like those we talked about earlier – a night light, warm bedclothes and so on may be enough to get things moving in the right direction.

There may be other ways of tackling this that might be worth thinking about:

- arrange your bedroom so your child can't come into your bed on the side they usually do

- try and alter your child's bedroom so that it is harder for them to get out of their bed or cot and then sneak into yours

- try putting a wedge under your door so the child can't push your door all the way open and get into your room while you are asleep

- if your little boy or girl sleeps in their own bed over at his or her grandparents, try making a change the night they come back

- be firm and stick to your guns. If they come into your room, take them back to their own bed quickly, quietly and without fuss.

- make sure they are comfortable; check temperature, add or take off a blanket, offer a small drink, take to toilet or change nappy if necessary, tuck in and go back to your own room.

- if your child keeps trying to come into your room you have to keep taking them back. You may have to be prepared to have a couple of sleepless nights before you get the child into the habit of staying in their own room. If there are two of you, take turns to take the child back to their room. Remember to keep eye contact to a minimum and make no comments.

Sometimes this can be a difficult behaviour to change. It can often build up over a period of time, particularly if a child has been ill and parents have taken them into their own bed to keep an eye on them and give them comfort. Later when the child is better they may refuse to leave. It is perhaps worth not letting the child get into the habit in the first place. Make their room as friendly and comfortable as possible with lots of their favourite things and look after them there if they are feeling a bit poorly. Make sure a little bit of light comes into the room or get a night light.

4 Feeding problems

Introduction

In many ways the problems that confront us in helping a child or young person to feed themselves, are similar to those that apply to toileting. One thing is clear with either situation – nagging or forcing does not work. As much as pinning a child to the potty and demanding they 'do something' will not produce good toilet habits, trying to pry open your child's mouth in order to insert a spoon will not help them eat properly. Sometimes without meaning to we can create feeding problems, because we are so anxious about our children not eating!

Feeding problems are not uncommon in pre-school children whether or not they have any form of special need. Some children seem to be remarkably healthy on surprisingly limited diets, consisting of things like yoghurts, biscuits, crisps and milk!

While this should give us some encouragement we need to think about what causes feeding difficulties for children with autism and what can keep the problems going. There are a number of things that can contribute to a feeding problem developing:

- some children are very sensitive to certain textures or flavours
- they may dislike anything with 'lumps'
- they may be very reluctant to use cutlery and feed themselves, and prefer to be fed by an adult

- many children are very 'faddy' about food
- the difficulty many children have about being flexible often applies to feeding, especially trying anything new
- many children are overactive and will find it hard to sit down and eat at a table.

Feeding problems may be maintained by:

- the opportunity to avoid an unwanted situation (sitting still, eating something that's not liked, or having to stop doing a preferred activity)
- getting attention for being disruptive at meal times.

Tackling the problems

Be realistic and take things in steps

If your child is unable to sit for more than five minutes at any task, you will not get from that point to sitting down for a full meal at the table in one go. Set realistic goals. A starting point might be 'Fred will sit at the table for five minutes'. Build up from this in stages.

What is the 'pay off' for the child?

You will also need to think about what the driving force is behind the behaviour. If for example your child is getting attention when they leave the table (perhaps you end up pursuing them around the house to try and get them to come back) the best solution may be to:

- ignore leaving the table so the child is given the minimum attenion for this
- give lots of praise and positive attention for 'good sitting' at the table and eating
- consider a 'no sitting, no food' rule. Be firm about all meals, snacks and drinks being taken when the child is seated.

But my child is not interested in food and screams if I try and make him sit at the table

First of all stay cool. Most children do not starve. Why not actually record how much your child actually eats over 24 hours, you may be very surprised.

There may be a number of possible strategies to tackling this.

Encourage 'good sitting'

Some children find being in close proximity to others in group situations, such as meal times, overwhelming. Try and understand this.

- Decrease the amount of time the child is expected to sit at the table. After a short period of 'good sitting' allow the child to get down and do a favourite activity.

- Do your best to ignore screaming. We know this is very hard, but the more attention you give to it the more the child will learn to use screaming to control your behaviour.

- Cut down on snacks between meals. Try not to give a child piles of their favourite junk food after they've just refused their dinner. Try fruit as a snack if they're hungry between meals.

- If they 'do a runner' from the table do not chase them (do you know many children who don't enjoy being chased at some point in their childhood?). Simply remove their food to prevent them grabbing a handful or spoonful and then running off. Replace the plate as and when they sit down.

Fussy eaters

- Gradually build up the amount and variety of food presented to your child.

- Do not force, nag or cajole.

Come on son, it's good enough for Desperate Dan!

- If the fussiness is due to a fixation on, or a dislike of particular tastes or textures, introduce new ones slowly. Try placing a small amount of new food (perhaps a few peas for example) on your child's plate separate from a favourite food.

- Try not to fuss, and do not feed your child or make a big deal about them eating.

- Give praise after food has been swallowed, not before.

- Tough it out. Don't give lots of attention even if food is chucked on the floor (put a plastic sheet under their chair if you need to).

- At the end of a meal just take the plate away without comment. Don't make a big fuss about what's been left.

- If you've tried to get your little boy or girl to try something new and it's been left, don't worry or fuss, just take the plate away.

- Try once a day at family meals to give a small quantity of what the family is eating. If the food is tried, give praise after it's swallowed. Remove what is left at the end of the meal. If necessary give a small quantity of what the child normally eats.

- Children behave differently in different places. They may eat happily at nursery but not at home, or the other way around. They may refuse food when they get a good reaction. Ever wonder why we struggle to get children to eat vegetables? Because we all freak out when they 'wont eat their greens'. Kids see our entertaining reaction and then the next time they see a spoonful of peas their mouth is shut tighter than a bank vault!

Other ideas

- Try and have regular routines around eating. Try to avoid having different arrangements for every one in the family.

- Think about using serving dishes or bowls of some kind. Give your child an empty plate and let them help themselves (younger children may need help). Seeing everyone else enjoy eating while they're sat in front of an empty plate, may make them think again about their decision to boycott tonight's offering, especially if they're hungry.

- The aim is not to stop hunger, make sure your child is hungry at meal times:

  - If necessary don't get sweets and biscuits in for a while (we know this is tough on other children in the family because it seems unfair, but weigh that against dealing with the temper tantrums that occur if they are there).

  - Cut down on snacks between meals

  - Wean your child off the bottle, some kids will not eat if they are full up with milk.

5 Self help

Introduction

It can be difficult teaching young children with autism how to take care of themselves. Sometimes they do not understand that they should dress themselves, even when they have the ability to do so. Dressing and undressing usually occur at very busy times of the day, so it can also be difficult finding the time to work on these skills at home.

Forward or backward chaining

Self help skills are best taught in small steps using a technique called forward or backward chaining. In forward chaining you teach the child the first step in the process and do the rest yourself. This would be used for something like tying a bow, You concentrate on teaching the first step in the process until the child can do it and then you teach the next step. It may take a long time to teach each step, but gradually the child manages to build up to tying a complete bow. In backward chaining, the child is taught the last step in the chain, for example when taking pants off you pull them down and your child pulls them off. You may have to hook his fingers under the waist of his pants and show him what to do. In this way, the child experiences some degree of success. It is also a good idea to say 'pants off', 'shoes off' or whatever is appropriate so that your child learns to respond to a request and knows exactly what is expected. It is important that everybody teaches the child in the same way, so this is another area where it is necessary to work closely with your child's teacher.

Teeth brushing/hair washing and cutting

Some children really dislike having their teeth cleaned. If this is a problem and you have tried various types of toothbrush and toothpaste, then take a deep breath, use a small brush and brush the teeth very quickly, rewarding the child immediately after with bubbles or some other non food treat. You could also try using a timer that rings after a few seconds. When your child is used to waiting for the ring and accepts a few seconds of tooth brushing, add a couple more seconds. Or break it down into small steps, using your finger to brush the teeth quickly with water, then when that is accepted add a tiny, tiny bit of toothpaste and gradually build up from there. There are no easy answers to this problem, and a quick daily battle even if your child really screams may be better than rotten teeth. Your child's resistance will pass and although you may find it exhausting and upsetting at the time, it is important to keep trying so that your child can develop independence and self confidence.

The same applies to hairwashing, although sting-free shampoo and lots of bubbles may make the task more pleasant. Use your child's interests to introduce distractions and rewards. Encourage them to wet their own hair in the bath, make foamy bubbles, or wash your hair as well as their own. Success in all these activities often comes when a child accepts them as part of the daily routine. And although it is difficult to keep calm when your child is distressed, if you can keep a sense of humour and be very matter-of-fact about it, you are already half way there.

Less frequent tasks such as nail cutting and hair cutting can also call for imaginative solutions. Parents often cut their children's hair while they are asleep; it may not be a very good haircut, but it is better than having a struggle with a pair of scissors or hair clippers. One parent (and others, no doubt) used to cut her son's finger and toe nails by biting them, because he was terrified of the scissors. He will now accept nail clippers as his fears have diminished over time.

Washing

Washing is another skill that requires a fairly organised approach so that your child understands the difference between serious washing and water play. Bath time, if your child enjoys the bath, can be a great play opportunity.

However, washing at the bathroom basin needs to be taught in the same step by step approach suggested above.

As has been said many times already, it is consistency that is so important. Your child will learn these skills in time if you remember these points:
- stick to your target and don't give up
- don't work on too many targets at once
- reward each success with loads of praise or whatever motivates your child best.

What usually happens is that after days or sometimes weeks of trying, your child will suddenly do what you want as though he knew how to do it all along. Don't forget to reward yourself as well as your child.

Step by step

Having a wash	tick when done

- [ ] pull up sleeves
- [ ] put plug in sink
- [ ] fill sink with water
- [ ] wet hands
- [ ] soap hands
- [ ] rinse hands
- [ ] squeeze out flannel
- [ ] soap flannel
- [ ] wash face
- [ ] rinse face
- [ ] squeeze out flannel
- [ ] pull out plug
- [ ] pick up towel
- [ ] dry face
- [ ] dry hands
- [ ] hang up towel
- [ ] pull down sleeves

Step by step

Getting undressed   **Tick when done**

☐ undo shoelaces
☐ remove left shoe
☐ remove right shoe
☐ pull left sock to heel
☐ pull off left sock
☐ pull right sock to heel
☐ pull off right sock

☐ pull trousers over bottom
☐ pull trousers to ankles
☐ pull out left leg
☐ pull out right leg

☐ pull up jumper
☐ take out left arm
☐ take out right arm
☐ pull over face
☐ pull over head

☐ pull up vest
☐ take out left arm
☐ take out right arm
☐ pull over face
☐ pull over head

☐ pull pants over bottom
☐ pull pants to ankles
☐ take out left foot
☐ take out right foot

Learning to play

Many children who have autism have very limited play skills and are unable to occupy themselves in the same way that young children often do. If you have a garden they may enjoy swinging, jumping on a trampoline and riding a bike. Indoors they may have favourite activities and occupy themselves happily with little need for variety. However, sometimes the most favourite activities are those that are difficult to cope with in a limited space. Children may go through stages where they want to throw things, jump on the furniture, scribble on the walls or play the same piece of video over and over again.

While trying to keep these activities at an acceptable level, it is helpful if you have some time to teach your child something new. Start with a toy they are interested in, maybe something they enjoy at school or nursery. Then spend a little time (about five minutes) each day teaching them to play with it. If it is a puzzle, you can use backward chaining to teach them, doing the puzzle yourself and asking them to put in the last piece, increasing the number of pieces they do as they become more skilled. Show them different things they can do with toy cars, teddies, duplo and so on. It is surprising how effective this can be over a period of time, and gradually the less desirable play will decrease.

Physical activity is also important, as research has shown that children who are given plenty of opportunity for running and playing active games are calmer and less likely to be aggressive*.

Looking after yourself

- It is helpful to write things down if you have the time, because a diary will show you just how much progress you and your child have made together.

- If your child is young and likes being touched it can be wonderful to lie down together while you give your child a massage. Lavender oil is very calming and many children enjoy having their hands, feet and back

* McGimsey and Favell (1988) 'The effects of increased physical exercise on disruptive behaviour in retarded persons'. *Journal of Autism and Developmental Disorders 18 pp 167-179.*

Kern et al (1982) 'The effects of physical exercise on self-stimulation and appropriate responding in autistic children' *Journal of Autism and Developmental Disorders 12 pp 399-419.*

rubbed with it. This has the added effect of making you feel very relaxed as well. Many chemists and health food shops sell small bottles of aromatherapy oils. Use a couple of drops of lavender mixed with almond oil.

- There are also some wonderful relaxing tapes you can buy or borrow from the library with music that washes over you and takes you to a tropical beach or a cool, green forest. Children quickly learn to associate the music with being relaxed and this is also a very effective remedy for a less than perfect day.

- Try to organise yourself a break or a special treat sometimes. Parents often remark that they feel guilty because they want to go on holiday and leave their autistic child behind with a relative. However, this may be just what you and the rest of your family need. Nurture any reasonable possibility for having some time to yourself. You will come back with more energy and everyone will benefit.

- If things are bad, ask for help. There are a list of organisations that will give advice in the back of this booklet. Voluntary groups and organisations run by parents are often the best place to start.

6 Coping with obsessional and repetitive behaviour

Introduction

Obsessions may include a range of interests and behaviour, for example, spinning, jumping, lining up cars, collecting shiny objects, adding up lines of numbers, repeatedly watching the credits on videos, wearing certain clothes and so on. Although obsessional behaviour may seem unimportant when your child is young, it sometimes prevents the development of new skills and interests and can become very disruptive to the whole family.

Keeping things manageable

Increasing your child's ability to play and communicate more effectively will give them alternatives to their repetitive behaviour. Ask their teacher, speech and language therapist, psychologist or an assistant at the local toy library to help you think of ways you may be able to develop and extend the activity. For example, obsessions with spinning objects may be developed into a range of play activities with cause and effect toys, which can also involve the important social skills of turn-taking and social interaction.

Obsessions with letters and numbers can be helpful in teaching early literacy and numeracy skills and hours spent lining up cars could be the beginning of some creative imaginative play. However, you must be prepared to meet with resistance and angry indignation if you start to change things too quickly. Watch at first, sitting near your child, and then begin by joining in briefly. As they accept your involvement in their activity, gradually introduce new things that they could do. For example, if your child spends a great deal of time lining up cars, you could develop this over several weeks.

Week 1: Watch, make comments, point to the different cars.
Week 2: Move cars a little out of line and 'brooom' them up and down.
Week 3: Put one or two cars in the garage.
Week 4: Move the cars around the garage.
Week 5 and 6: Introduce ramps, roads, bridges. Have fun!

Self-stimulatory behaviour

If your child flaps their hands, spins, rocks or races up and down the room in a constant frenzy of activity, it will take considerable energy on your part to keep this behaviour at an acceptable level. Children with autism often do these things because they enjoy the sensation, but it also keeps them feeling calm and safe, so if you are going to stop them doing it, you will have to give them some more acceptable activity to do instead.

For example, if your child spins or flaps their hands, ignore it at times when you are too busy to distract them to other activities but don't allow it at other times of the day when you have time to do things together. If they like watching videos, and you have time to sit with them, don't let them spin or flap while they are watching. Be very firm about it and turn the video off when they start. Say firmly 'no spinning' and show by gesture what you mean. Build up a schedule over a period of about six weeks when the amount of spinning that they are allowed to do gradually decreases each week until it becomes part of their daily routine; when they come in from school for example, or when they are going to bed. You could allow it as a form of relaxation when your child is tired or unhappy, or use it as a reward for finishing something less exciting.

5, 4, 3, 2, 1......
... STOP!

Allocate time for spinning

Other preoccupations

Some children have collections which are kept in a certain place or are carried around. These may sometimes grow so large they interfere with the daily routine. Again, draw up a schedule that takes you through the withdrawal process week by week. Reduce the collection by removing one item each week.

Obsessions with talking about only one topic can be dealt with in the same way. Start by choosing a time when that subject is not allowed, for example at mealtimes (if your child is happy to eat) or when watching television. Gradually increase the number of places and times when that topic of conversation is not allowed. It also helps to develop your child's knowledge about their favourite subject of conversation and broaden their perspective so that it also becomes a useful teaching tool. Using a timer with a loud ring can be useful in controlling obsessional behaviour, particularly for children with severe learning difficulties. It can be used to time the amount of time allowed for spinning or talking (for example), or it can be used to time the gaps in between.

Sometimes children will stop a repetitive behaviour if you join in and do it with them, or attempt to change it into a game. You may not want to do this, but it is often very effective and well worth a try.

Unpleasant, destructive or dangerous behaviour

Introduction

This category covers a wide range of behaviour including spitting, chewing clothes into holes, tearing wallpaper off the walls, or throwing objects without any thought of where they might land. Worried parents have been horrified to find their child has lit the gas at 5 am in order to make breakfast or run a bath of boiling water in the middle of the night after wetting the bed. In all these cases the strategy will depend to some extent on your circumstances, how energetic you feel and how well your child responds to things like rewards, praise, and so on. Children with very severe learning difficulties or children who are hyperactive will need a different approach to children who are fairly calm and have other interests.

Ask yourself some questions

- How do I, and others in the family, respond to the behaviour?
- Is this behaviour for attention?
- Does my child do this to relax?
- Is it a habit they do because they like doing it?
- What things could my child do instead?
- Could I prevent the behaviour by changing the environment or the way we do things?
- Is the behaviour a result of things my child finds difficult?
  For example, change of routine, loud noises, extreme heat or cold, too much excitement?

Diaries

If you are not sure of the answers to these questions, keep a diary and write down each time the behaviour occurs. If it is very frequent write the time in 5, 15 or 30 minute intervals down the side of the sheet of paper and tick the time the behaviour is worse. You can then see if there is any pattern. If children spend a lot of time jumping on the furniture between 7-10 in the evening, they may need some exercise just before that time. An exercise bike, trampoline, old sofa or a run round the block may be a good substitute. Make sure your child has regular opportunities for exercise throughout the day, as this will have an overall effect on improving behaviour.

When you are trying to work out good strategies to use to help your child, it is wise to involve all the important adults and older children in a brainstorming activity. Look at your child's strengths and interests as these can often be used as rewards or distractors.

A combination of solutions

Strategies are often approached on two or three levels so that you may have more success using a combination of solutions. For example:

One strategy that can be used for dangerous behaviour is to secure the environment. Put a lock on the kitchen door if your child gets up early but at the same time leave a snack in your child's room so they will be less likely to want to cook themselves breakfast. If your child jumps off the furniture on to a glass-topped coffee table, then for the time being the coffee table will have to go and the furniture rearranged to make jumping a little more difficult. At the same time you may decide to always say 'no jumping' when your child jumps, and to offer another activity which could be something they enjoy like listening to music through the headphones, or something physical like swinging or riding a bike. You may decide to buy a trampoline or an old sofa and let your child jump safely on that.

If your child chews holes in their clothes it is often best to take a firm approach and say 'out of mouth' each time you see them doing it, taking the clothes out of their mouth so they learn to associate that phrase and to understand that it means 'no chewing'. If you do this it is very important that everybody does it and you give your child something else to do instead.

If they only do it at certain times of the day, for example in the evening while watching a video, you may decide to put them in old clothes and ignore the chewing, or you may decide to turn off the video every time the chewing starts.

You could also substitute another activity your child could do instead of chewing their clothes. If you could stand the mess, water play or painting are two activities that are relaxing and absorbing for young children and would prevent them chewing. Waterproof aprons are also very tough and stiff – not at all chewable. Some children refuse to wear them but they do give a possible solution. You could dress your child in very strong fabrics that don't tear easily such as denim or you may prefer to take a more gentle approach and substitute something more acceptable to chew such as a very hard rusk or a soft toy made with vinyl or leather. If you decide on the last course of action you will then have to build in gradually times your child is not allowed to chew so that they chew for less time until they are not chewing at all. This is quite important if you do not want your child to be still chewing inappropriately as they get older.

Children who spit will often stop very quickly if they are calmly asked to clean it up. This may mean holding the tissue in their hand with your hand over the top to clean up the mess, or giving their mouth a good wipe. Never show shock or disgust even when it has landed on your face, as that almost always makes the problem much worse. Just say, 'no spitting' and 'clean it up'.

One child who, for no obvious medical reason, suddenly started pulling down his pants and weeing anywhere was stopped from doing this by simply dressing him in dungarees or overalls. While he was attempting to undo the straps somebody would notice and take him to the toilet. Outside with his coat on he couldn't reach the straps, so providing he was offered a chance to go to the toilet regularly, he gradually forgot his habit and began to use the toilet again in the proper way. After five or six weeks the dungarees were no longer needed.

Most problems need a similar approach to those described above. You can:

- alter the environment to make it harder for your child to be destructive
- substitute something similar but less harmful
- offer your child another activity that is exciting but makes it impossible for them to do anything less acceptable at the same time
- tell them not to do it using the same short phrase and physically stop the behaviour eg, 'No throwing' and take away what they were about to throw
- try to make sure your child has plenty of opportunities to exercise
- if anything particularly seems to trigger the behaviour, try to change or alter it by changing your routine, or avoiding certain situations
- you can use 'overcorrection' eg, make them clean up the mess if they tip or throw something. You will at first have to do it with them, guiding their hand
- help your child relax at stressful times by massaging hands, feet or back with lavender oil, rocking together, playing soothing music, having a warm bath, breathing deeply and relaxing. All these things will help you as well
- praise or reward your child if they stop when you ask them to
- try to keep calm. Use short requests. If you get angry it is like a red rag to a bull and the behaviour will become much more difficult to deal with.

Time out

This is a technique used by many parents and is usually a simple 'Go to your room'. With an autistic child this approach is much more complicated. They may not understand why they are being sent to their room and they may become more destructive in their room where you can't see them. However, if they are doing something unacceptable and you are sure they are doing it for attention, then sending them to their room for a very short time (up to five minutes for a young child) can be a good solution now and then when you have tried everything else without success. If their room is safe, and you can relax, it will give you both an opportunity to calm down.

Aggressive behaviour

Some children with autism have a lot of difficulty being with other children or with adults. They find them unpredictable and frightening as they are not able to understand why they behave as they do. Like all children, they may also be jealous of siblings but will not have the language skills to help them talk about it. Other things that sometimes result in aggressive behaviour are sensitivity to certain types of touch, certain sounds (some that we may not even notice) and certain colours or shades of light and dark. Changes of routine may cause despair or fury, as will more specific things like something being moved from a straight line. For example, a child once became very distressed and angry when the crisp packet he had laid carefully on a particular spot on the ground outside kept moving in the breeze. Some children become so distressed they lash out at anybody and are difficult to calm. Others may push, poke, pull hair or bite. Unfortunately, aggressive behaviour can be very difficult to change in a short space of time particularly in children with very limited means of communication. The two most important things to do are:

1 respond calmly
2 try to find out what is causing the behaviour.

Respond calmly

A behaviour that begins innocently as a response to a problem can become very entrenched if the child learns that it causes a great deal of excitement. It then becomes a habit that is difficult to break, It is also important to remember that children may be aggressive because they feel distressed. It is better to respond in a very calm manner to avoid making the child more anxious and making their behaviour more difficult.

Find out the cause of the behaviour

You may have to keep a diary in order to reach an understanding of why the behaviour occurs. The most common reasons are given here with examples of different strategies. However, what you decide to do will depend on your knowledge of your child.

● **Your child is using the behaviour to communicate**

Many two year old children ask 'why' all the time. Children with communication difficulties have to accept many things they do not understand. It is not surprising that they sometimes use physical and unsociable means of communication. Aggressive behaviour is guaranteed to produce a response.

If you think this is the main reason your child is aggressive then it is important to work with your child's teacher to help teach alternative communication skills. Your child may learn to sign essential words like 'help' or to use symbols or gestures. If they have no speech, it is important that they learn to make choices by pointing or choosing symbols and pictures. They will feel more in control and less likely to lash out in anger or frustration.

- **Your child is using aggression to avoid something she doesn't want to do.**

If your child hits her sister whenever she has to tidy up her toys she may be trying to cause a distraction that will result in the task being done for her. The best response is to say firmly 'no hitting' and remove your child from the situation for a couple of minutes. Don't look or give any attention to her whatsoever. Comfort the other child and then take the culprit back to finish tidying up. Stay with her in case it happens again. If necessary, help your child pick up the toys by holding your hand over their's and guiding it. Give lots of praise when the task is finished.

- **Your child is using aggression in order to gain attention**

As above, say firmly 'no hitting' and don't say anything else. Take them away without looking at them or giving any attention and sit them somewhere quiet for up to five minutes. Take them back to what they were doing and don't say anything else. Give lots of praise when they are behaving well.

If your child scratches or hits you when you are on the phone or doing something that you can't leave, like changing the baby, you may have to think of other strategies to deal with it. Distract your child with a favourite toy or activity before the behaviour becomes aggressive or find a way of letting your child join in. Maybe they would like to play with playdough while you prepare the dinner or bath their baby doll while the baby is having a bath.

- **Your child is unable to share or take turns with others**

Children with autism find it hard to understand why they have to share or why they have to wait their turn. These are skills that should be worked on at school and at home and progress may seem slow at times. However, children learn and it is important to introduce turn-taking into games at a very early age.

- **Your child is reacting to something they find frightening or irritating**

Children with autism may be very sensitive to certain sounds and certain kinds of touch. They may find some perfectly ordinary events really scary but they are not able to say why. Some children put their hands over their ears as though they are in pain. Ear plugs may help to block out sounds that children find distressing. If children find certain textures difficult to touch, it is best to avoid them for a while and reintroduce them gently. Sometimes children have panic attacks and may become very aggressive. It is important to be calm and matter-of-fact, talk calmly to your child and try to prevent them hurting themselves or hurting you. Regular exercise and relaxation are both effective in helping children keep calm.

8 Self injury

Introduction

Self injury includes: head banging, a child slapping or hitting themselves, biting themselves, poking or gouging at their eyes, and pulling at their hair.

Self injury is one of the most distressing and difficult types of behaviour for parents and carers to deal with. By its very nature such behaviour damages the child in some way, and it is this aspect that makes it so difficult to understand or sympathise with.

With this particular variety of behaviour it is important for parents to seek support and advice from the professional community.

The ideas and principles behind dealing with this type of behaviour are the same or very similar to the ones we have outlined elsewhere when discussing other behaviour problems. It is important to respond rapidly, effectively and consistently to self injury and to ask ourselves a series of questions.

What is my child trying to communicate through this behaviour?

We may not always find out a clear answer to this question but if you can come up with some ideas it may help you teach your child alternative and more appropriate ways of communicating their needs.

How do I begin to tackle this behaviour?

One of the first steps is to think about the context: when and where does it happen? What is going on in the environment? There can be a number of triggers for self injury:

- noise which your child can find overwhelming and distressing
- particular aspects of personal hygiene which are experienced by your child as intrusive and very uncomfortable such as; brushing teeth, washing and brushing or combing hair
- seeking to avoid demands and control situations
- frustration at not being able to communicate needs or feelings
- wanting to be left alone.

When a child screams and bangs their head in a noisy classroom, or bites themselves as soon as hot water or shampoo makes contact with their hair the motivation behind the behaviour is very clear. The child is telling us 'I hate this' or 'It's too loud for me in here'. When we understand this we can begin to make changes to make the situation more tolerable. We can try if possible to help them communicate their distress at loud noises by signing or saying 'too loud', or putting their hands over their ears. This can be a cue for parents, teachers or carers to remove them to a quieter and less stressful environment.

We can also try and teach children the skills to carry out as much of their own personal hygiene as possible so they are not having their personal space invaded by others more than necessary. They may take time to learn how to brush their teeth, and they may not like it much at first, but it may be much more acceptable then having someone else stick a toothbrush in their mouth. If they can do it themselves they will at least be in control.

But what about times when we can't understand why they're doing it?

Sometimes it isn't obvious, and there are no quick fix solutions. Parents, teachers and carers have to carefully observe and watch what is happening when the behaviour is going on. This may give them clues as to why the behaviour is happening.

But ignoring the behaviour is not an option this time is it?

No it isn't. We must think carefully however about how we react. Young children may not be able to tell the difference between good and bad attention. Reactions of fear, anger, surprise may reinforce the behaviour.

A child should be given minimum attention for self-injury, and given a short clear and firm verbal message such as 'No head banging'. Rewards for appropriate behaviour can be things like hugs and kisses and praise, or tangible rewards like food, drinks, or toys.

As much attention as possible should be given to your child when they are not self injuring. It is especially important to give attention to your child when they are using words, signs, pointing or gesture to communicate their needs.

Self injury can be caused by physical discomfort, illness or pain. If it is not clear why this behaviour is happening a full physical examination by a doctor may help.

Summary

Self injury is a difficult thing to tackle but there are ways of dealing with it. It needs to be responded to rapidly and consistently and your child must not get any rewards for the behaviour. Keep the attention given to a minimum. Give lots of attention for positive behaviour. Distraction may help prevent self injury, especially if you know there are times in the day which will be difficult for your child to cope with because of the number of people, the level of noise etc. Perhaps give them a favourite toy to hold, or give them some time in a quiet place. Teach them to indicate that they are upset or frustrated. Learn to recognise the signs.

Above all, if you are finding it tough to manage, get help.

Useful organisations

The National Autistic Society
Head Office
393 City Road
London EC1 1NG
Tel: 020 7833 2299
Fax: 020 7833 9666
Email: nas@nas.org.uk   Website: www.info.autism.org.uk

Autism Helpline: 0845 070 4004 Minicom 020 7903 3597
This is a written and telephone enquiry service with the phone line open
Monday – Friday 10am – 4pm – offers advice and support to parents, carers
and people with autism and Asperger syndrome.
Email: autismhelpline@nas.org.uk

Fundraising: 020 7903 3559
Email: fundraising@nas.or.uk

Information: 0845 70 4004
This is a written and telephone enquiry service with the phone lines open
between 10 am and 2 pm weekdays – offers information and advice on all
aspects of autism, NAS Services and related topics to professionals, students,
researchers, voluntary organisations. In addition there is a library that parents
and researchers can use by appointment only.
Email: informationcentre@nas.org.uk
Online orders: www.autism.org.uk/infosheets

Press: 0207903 3593
Email: press@nas.org.uk

Prospects: Supported Employment Service: 020 7704 7450
Prospects is a supported employment service for adults with autism and
Asperger syndrome. Email: prospects@nas.org.uk

Publications: 0207903 3595
The Publications Department has one of the best lists on autism and Asperger
syndrome in the country. Catalogues will be sent out on request.
Email: publications@nas.org.uk Online orders: www/autism.org.uk/pubs

Services Division – for details of NAS schools and adult centres
Church House, Church Road, Filton
Bristol BS34 7BD
Tel: 0117 974 8400
Fax: 0117 987 2576
Email: services@nas.org.uk

Development and Outreach and Training
Castle Heights, 4th Floor, 72 Maid Marian Way, Nottingham NG1 6BJ
Tel: 0115 911 3360
Fax: 0115 911 2259
Email: development@nas.org.uk

Training
Tel: 0115 911 3363 or 3367
Fax: 0115 911 3362
Training Services offers various courses for parents and professionals relating to the autistic spectrum. Tailor-made courses are also available to groups.
Email: training@nas.org.uk
        Conference@nas.org.uk

Volunteering Network
Tel: 0115 911 3369
Fax: 0115 911 3362
The Volunteering Network co-ordinates nationwide parent to parent and befriending schemes. The schemes are available to parents of people with autistic spectrum disorders.
Email: volunteering@nas.org.uk

The NAS Centre for Social and Communication Disorders
Elliot House, 113 Masons Hill, Bromley, Kent BR2 9HT
Tel: 020 466 0098
Fax: 020 466 0118

MENCAP
HQ 123 Golden Lane, London EC1Y ORT
Tel: 020 7454 0454
Gives a wide range of information and advice on many subjects including toileting aids and holiday accommodation for children and adults with severe learning difficulties.

Carers National Association
20/25 Glasshouse Yard, London EC1A 4JS
Tel: 020 490 8818

Contact a Family
209 – 211 City Road, London, EC1A 1 JN
Tel 020 7608 8700
Puts families of children with special needs in touch with one another and provides support and advice for them.
Website: www.cafamily.org.uk

Crossroads
10 Regent Place Rugby, Warwickshire CV21 2PN
Tel. 01788 573653
Offers support and information for people who care for a disabled child or adult at home.

Professional help
If you need help, your first step is to speak to your GP who is able to refer you on to a clincal psychologist. Alternatively, your local health authority may be able to suggest someone who could help you. You can also find out the details of your local parent support group (contact The National Autistic Society Helpline) and speak to other parents. They may well know of a professional in your area who they found to be really helpful.

Books and pamphlets
Recommended Reading

The autistic spectrum – a parent's guide (1998)
The National Autistic Society.*
This pack has been put together specifically for parents and carers of children recently diagnosed with an autistic spectrum disorder. It is designed to answer some of the questions parents may have including recognising the signs, education, financial help.

Tony Attwood (1993) *Why Does Chris do That?*
The National Autistic Society *
A booklet that describes the causes of some behaviour in children with autism or Asperger syndrome and suggests some strategies to help manage them.

Tony Attwood (1997) *Asperger syndrome: a guide for parents and professionals* *
This book provides a description and analysis of the unusual charactersitics associated with Asperger syndrome and outlines practical strategies.

Simon Baron-Cohen and Patrick Bolton (1993) *Autism: the facts**
This book explains autism in a way which is understandable, supportive and helpful.

Maria Wheeler (1999) *Toilet training for individuals with autism and related disorders: a comprehensive guide for parents and teachers*
Jessica Kingsley Publishers*
over 200 toilet training tips and more than 40 case examples with solutions.

Philip Whitaker (2001) *Challenging behaviour and autism: making sense – making progress*
The National Autistic Society*
Practical strategies for preventing or managing the sorts of challenging behaviour most likely to be ecountered.

Peter Vermeulen (2001) *Autistic thinking – this is the title*
Jessica Kingsley Publishers*
This book has an original approach that evokes an appreciation for the strengths of the autism mind.

Louise Gorrod (1997) *My brother is different*.
The National Autistic Society*
Written by a mother of an autistic child and illustrated in full colour this booklet explains an autistic child's behaviour in terms that young siblings will be able to understand, enabling them to deal both practically and emotionally with their brother/sister. Aimed at children around 5-8 year age range.

Martine Ives and Neil Munro (2002) *Caring for a child with autism*
Jessica Kingsley Publishers*
This full and readable guide answers the questions often asked by parents and carers after a diagnosis of auttism.

Leicestershire County Council and Fosse Health Trust (1998) *Autism: how to help your young child*. The National Autistic Society*
This practical booklet is divided into three areas where difficulties may arise for a child with autism; social interaction, communication and imagination. The booklet includes an index of pen-pictures to help parents find their child among the examples and directs them to the relevant section. Each section is then divided into 'What to look out for', followed by 'Things to try' to help the child's behaviour.

Liz Hannah (2001) *Teaching young children with autism spectrum disorders: a practical guide for parents and staff in mainstream schools and nurseries*
The National Autistic Society*
This wide-ranging, well-illustrated book offers all kinds of tired and tested strategies to help young people with autistic spectrum disorders develop and learn.

Penny Barratt et al. (2001) *Developing pupils' social communication skills*
David Fulton*
This book offers dozens of simple but highly effective strategies for developing communication and social skills.

Lorna Wing (1996) *The Autistic Spectrum*: *A guide for Parents and Professionals** Constable
This book describes what autism is, how to help those with the condition, and the services available. A good guide for parents and anyone working with people with autism.

* *all books marked with this asterisk are available from The National Autistic Society's*
  Publications Department. Tel 0171 903 3595
  Online orders: www.autism.org.uk/pubs

References

N Dalyrymple and L Rube (1992) Toilet training and behaviours of people with autism: parents' views. *Journal of Autism and Developmental Disorders*, 22(2), 265–275

Susan Dodd (1994) *Managing Problem Behaviours: A practical guide for parents and teachers of young children with special needs*
Maclennan and Petty
An easy to follow book covering a wide range of problem behaviours.

R Wayne Gilpin (1993) *Laughing and loving with autism.*
Future Education Inc.
This is a collection of humorous stories written by parents, other family members, friends and teachers of children and adultsfrom all over America.

Patricia Howlin and Michael Ruttler (1989) *Treatment of Autistic Children*
John Wiley and Sons. Aimed mainly at professionals,this book has an excellent chapter on coping with obsessive behaviours as well as many other suggestions for dealing with problem behaviours in children with autism.

Eric Schopler, Editor (1995) *Parent Survival Manual: a Guide to Crisis Resolution in Autism and Related Developmental Disorders*, Plenum Press*
An American book giving a broad collection of strategies that parents have found successful in dealing with difficult and challenging behaviours.

Further reading

*Cumine V., Leach J. and Stevenson G. (2000) Autism in the early years. London: David Fulton. 1853465992

*Carol Gray (2002)My social stories book. London: Jessica Kingsley. Autistic Society. 1 85302 950 5

*Hannah L. (2001) Teaching young children with autistic spectrum disorders: a practical guide for parents and staff in mainstream schools and nurseries. London: The National Autistic Society. 1899280324

*Leicestershire County Council and Fosse Health Trust (1998) Autism: how to help your young child. London: The National Autistic Society. 1899280650

*Moor J. (2002) Playing, laughing and learning with children on the autism spectrum: a practical resource of play ideas for parents and carers. London: Jessica Kingsley. 1843100606

*The National Autistic Society (1998) The autistic spectrum - a parent's guide. London: The National Autistic Society. 1 899280081

*Jennifer L. Savner and Brenda Smith Myles (2000) Making visual supports work in the home and community: strategies for individuals with autism and Asperger syndrome. Shawne Mission, Kansas: Autism Asperger Publishing Co. 0 967 2514 6 X

*Enuresis Resource and Information Centre (2002) 'We can do it!' Helping children who have learning disabilities with bowel and bladder management: a guide for parents. Bristol: Enuresis Resource and Information Centre. 1 903444 19 5

*Wing L. (1996) The autistic spectrum: a guide for parents and professionals. London: Constable. 1 84119 674 6

*Available from NAS Publications
Tel 020 7903 3595
www.nas.org.uk/pubs

Finally

Between us we've notched up quite a lot of years working with autistic children. Nevertheless we both still come across children who throw us completely! We have to rack our brains and think of some way to get a situation unstuck. There have been times when the two of us have sat in a car outside of one of our offices, having just visited a school or a family, wondering quite what to do next. In this way we can share, in a small way, the sense of frustration and being at a loss, that many families live with day by day as they try and bring up their autistic children, and prepare them for a world these young people will continue to find confusing and frightening.

With any of the problems your child may have, you may too, find yourself stumped for ideas, and feel you have tried everything. There are professionals to help you if you need them. It may help to talk to one of them. Other parents may also be able to help; they may have a simple idea to try, or be able to think with you about modifying the strategies you have already tried. Your doctor or paediatrician may be able to advise you about medical treatments if your child is showing hyperactivity as well as autism.

We hope that what we've written may help in some small way, and make life just a little bit easier. Above all if you can believe that you are not entirely alone, and there are other parents, voluntary organisations, and even some professionals (!) who do understand and want to help, we have achieved a lot.

We wish you all the best.